AF353159

KIDS MEDICAL
ABC Book 2

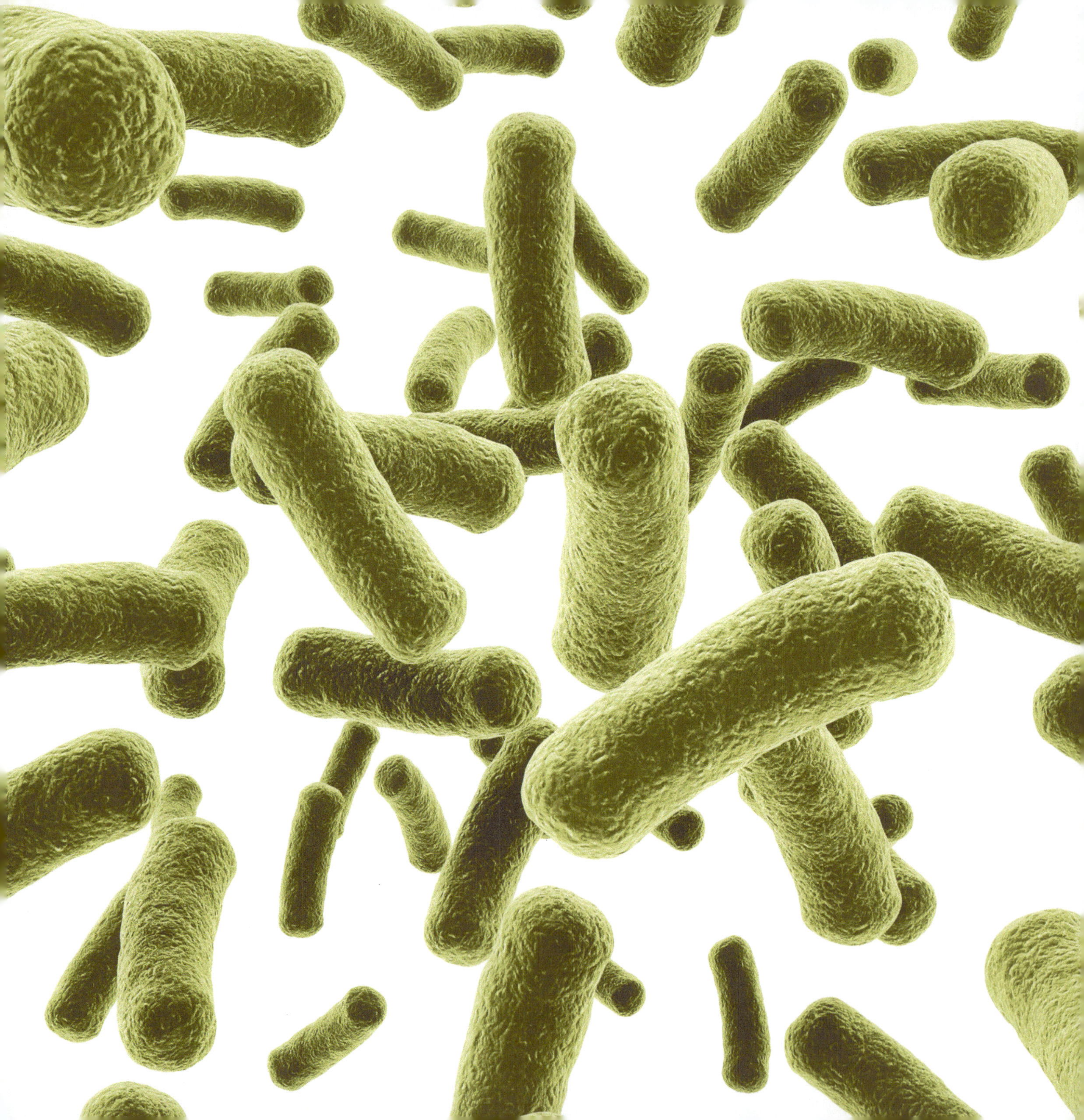

**www.LittleGalileoBooks.com**

# KIDS MEDICAL

## ABC Book 2

by Roy Jelinek

# A   Arm

The flexible upper limbs extending from the shoulder to the hands.

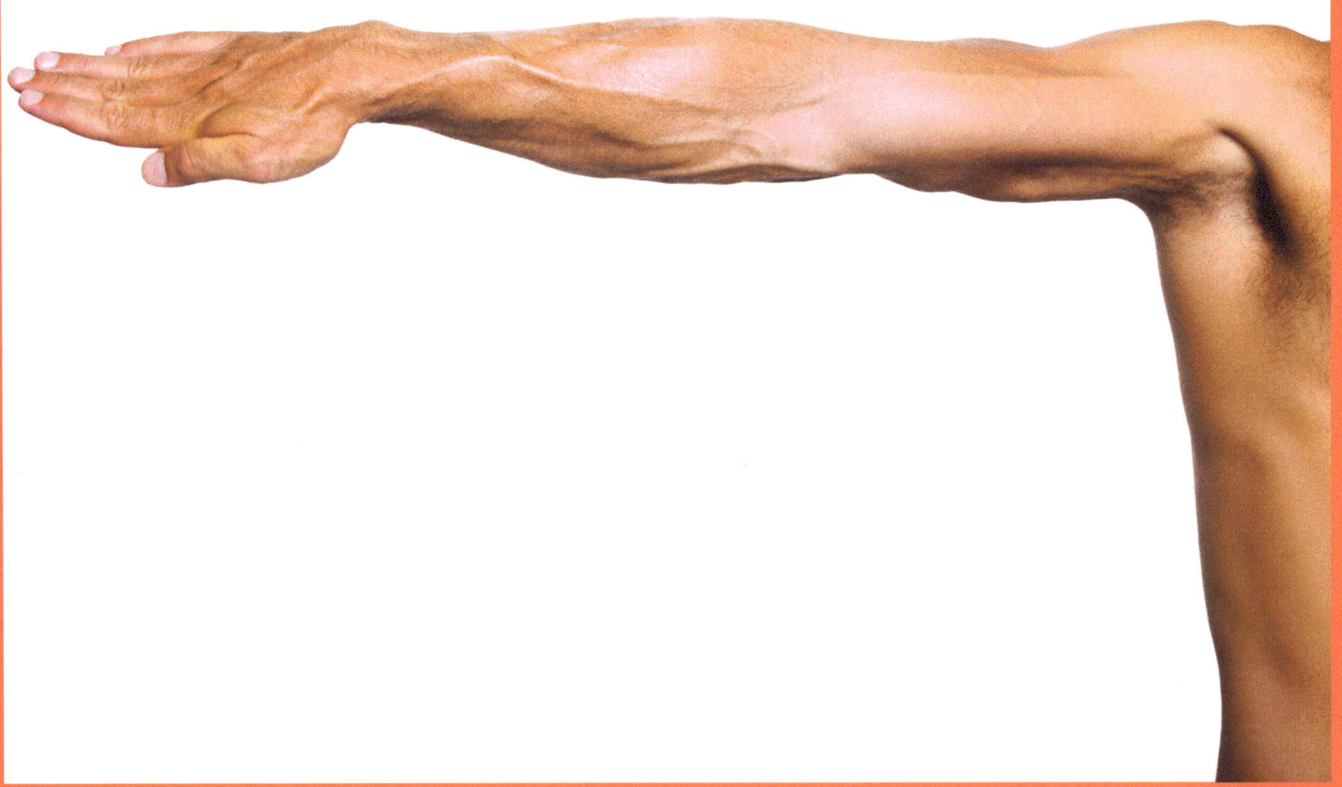

# B   Blood Pressure

Measurement of the force of blood pressing against the walls of arteries.

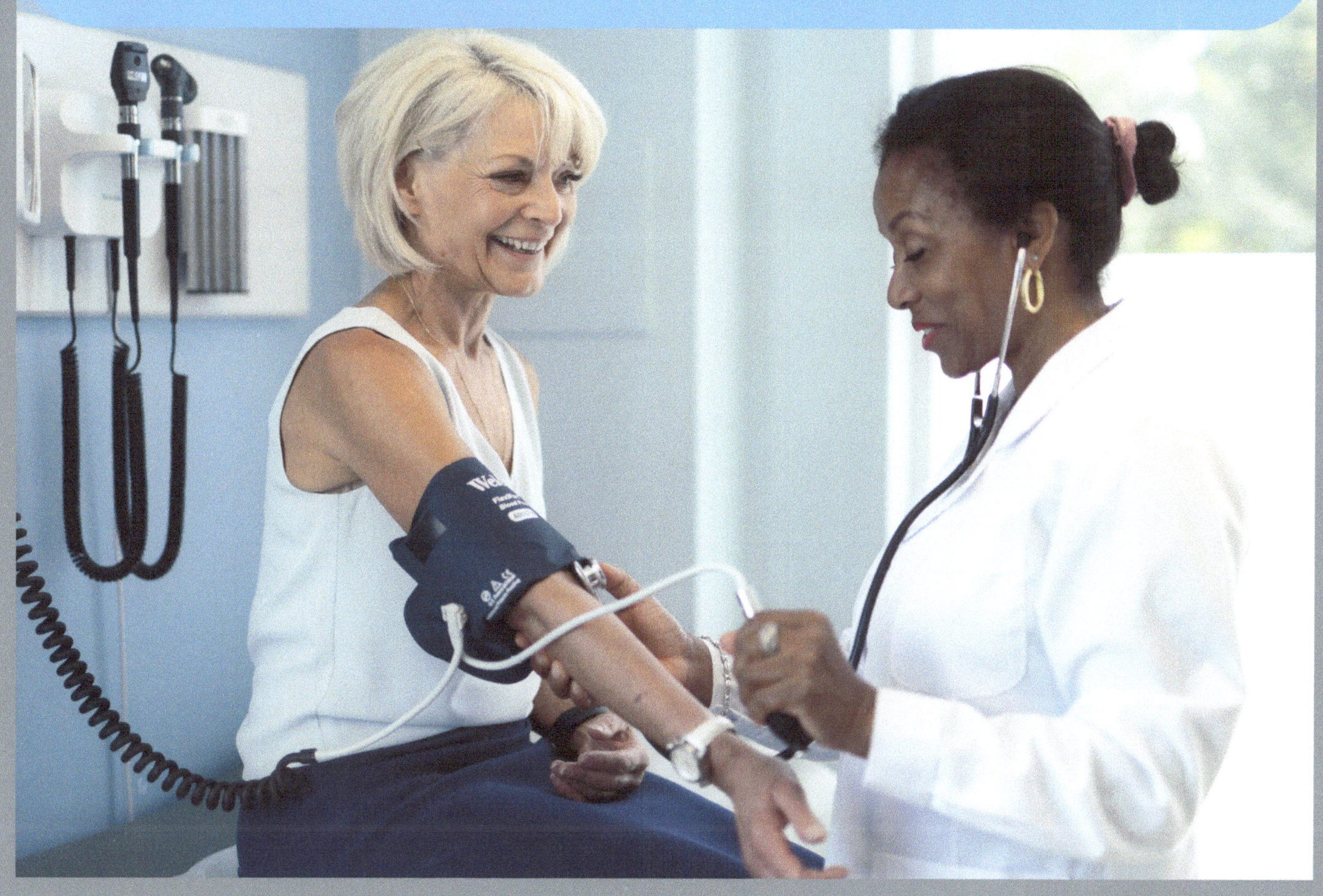

# C  Cough

A sudden expulsion of air from the lungs in order to clear them.

# D  Dentist

A medical professional who cares for teeth, gums and oral health.

# E  Ear Ache

Pain felt in the the ear often caused by an infection or injury.

# F   First Aid

Immediate care given to the ill or injured before full medical treatment.

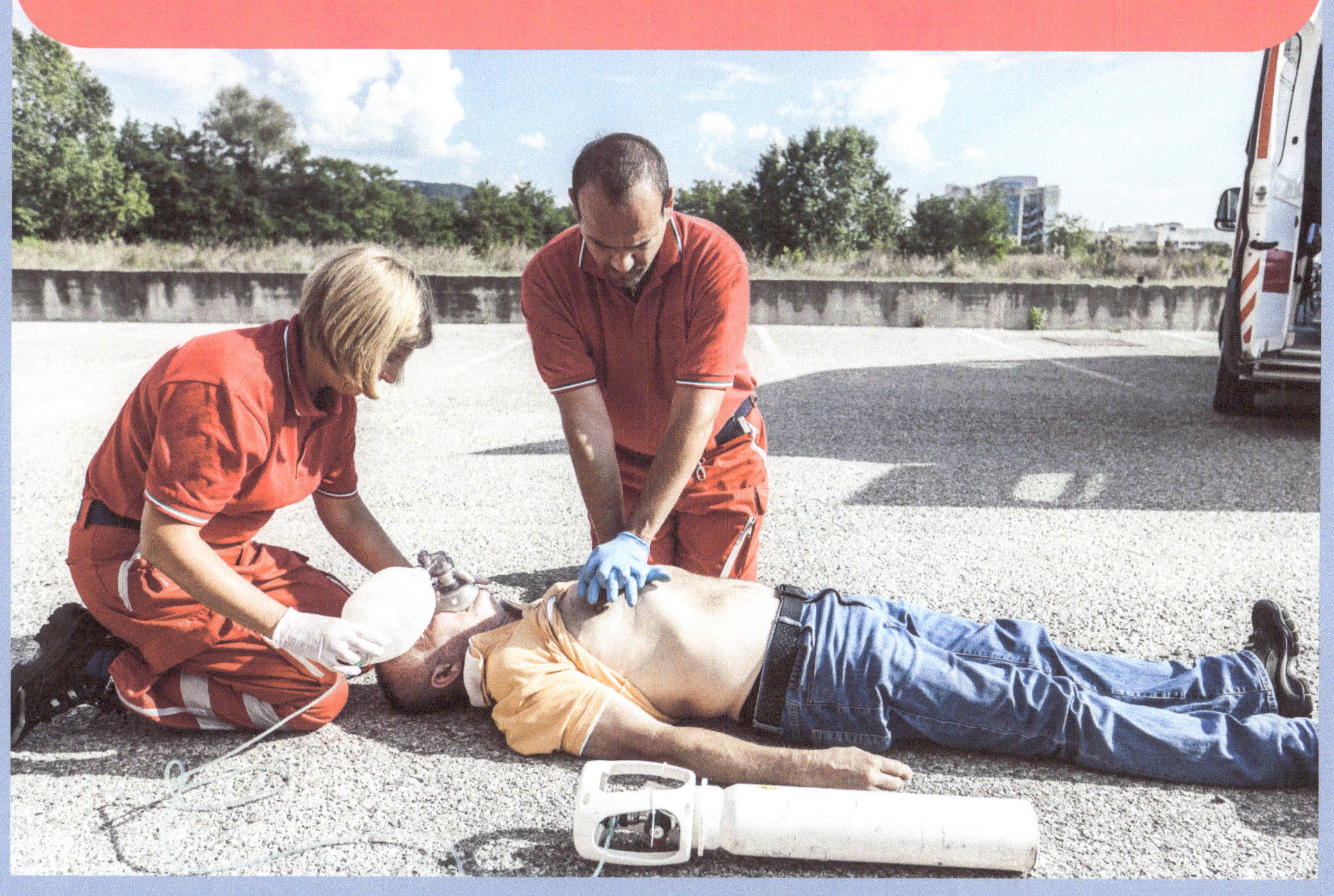

# G  Germs

Microscopic organisms which can cause infection, illness and disease.

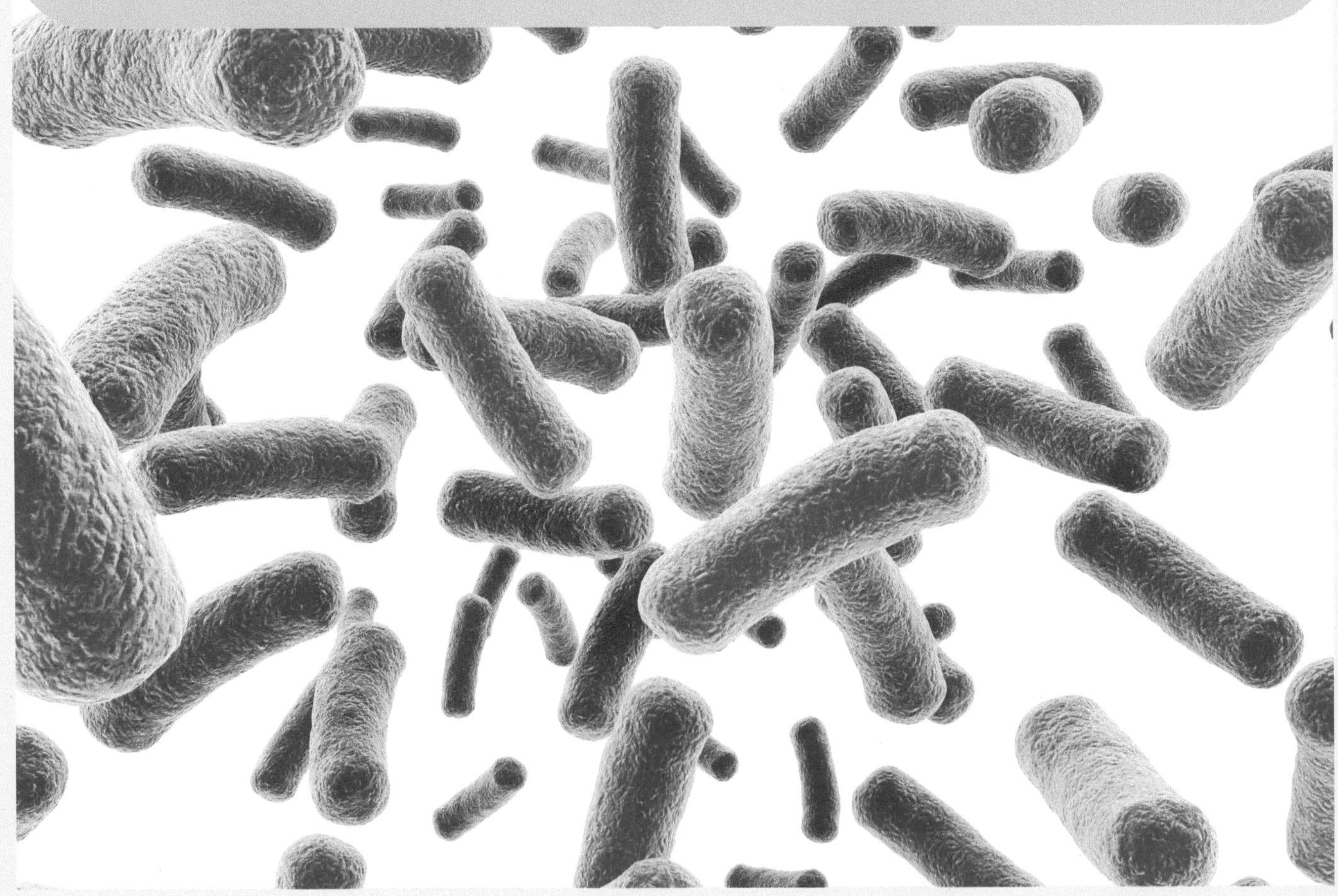

# H  Headache

Discomfort or pain to any part of the head, scalp or neck areas.

# I  Immunity

The body's natural ability to fight off illness, infection and disease.

# J  Jaundice

A yellowing of the skin and eyes due to blood imbalance and the liver.

# K  Knees

The joint which connects the thigh bone to the lower leg bone.

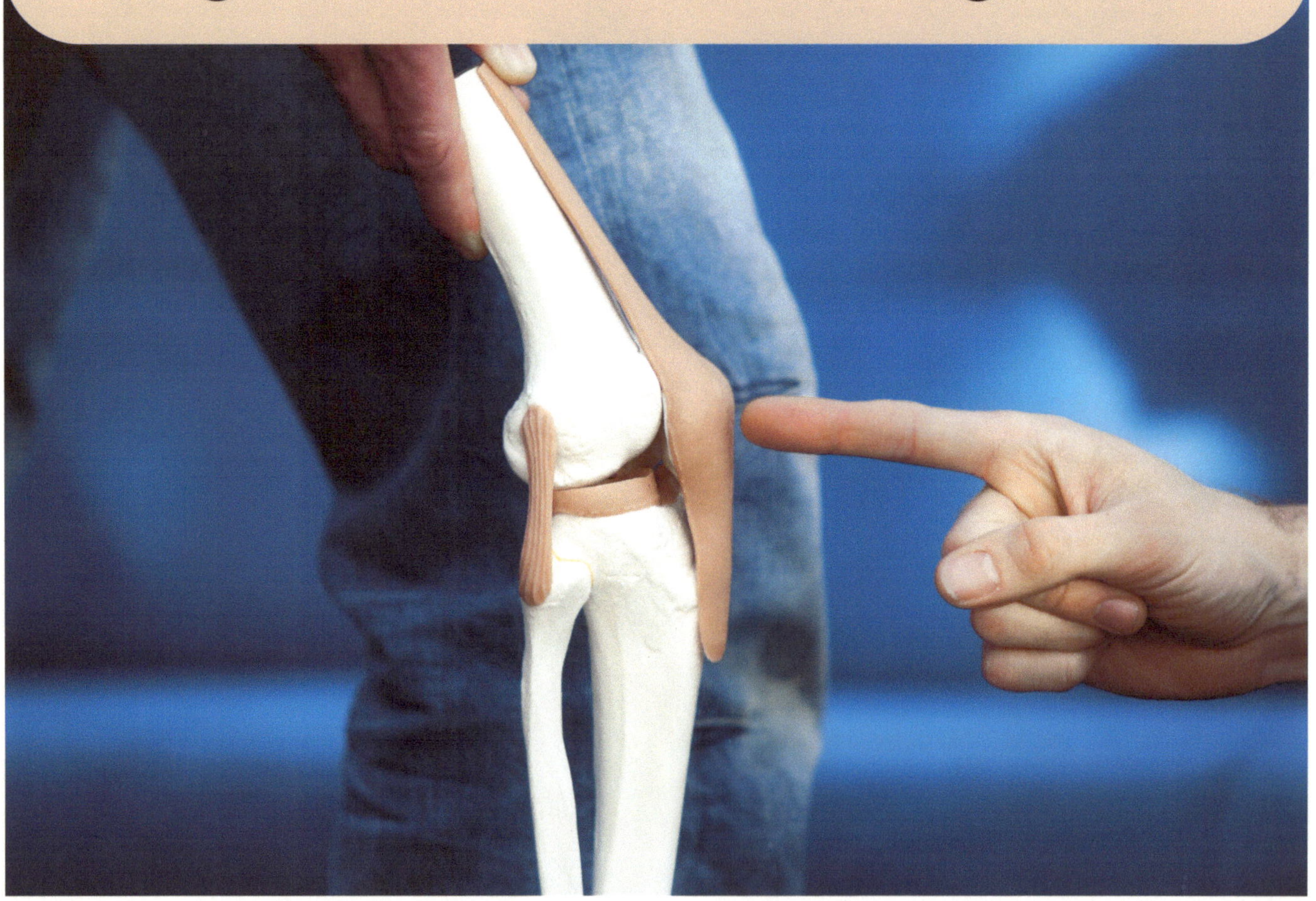

# L  Lotion

A cream applied to skin for medicinal, moisturizing or sun protection.

# M  Muscle

A bundle of fibers which can relax or contract to create body movement.

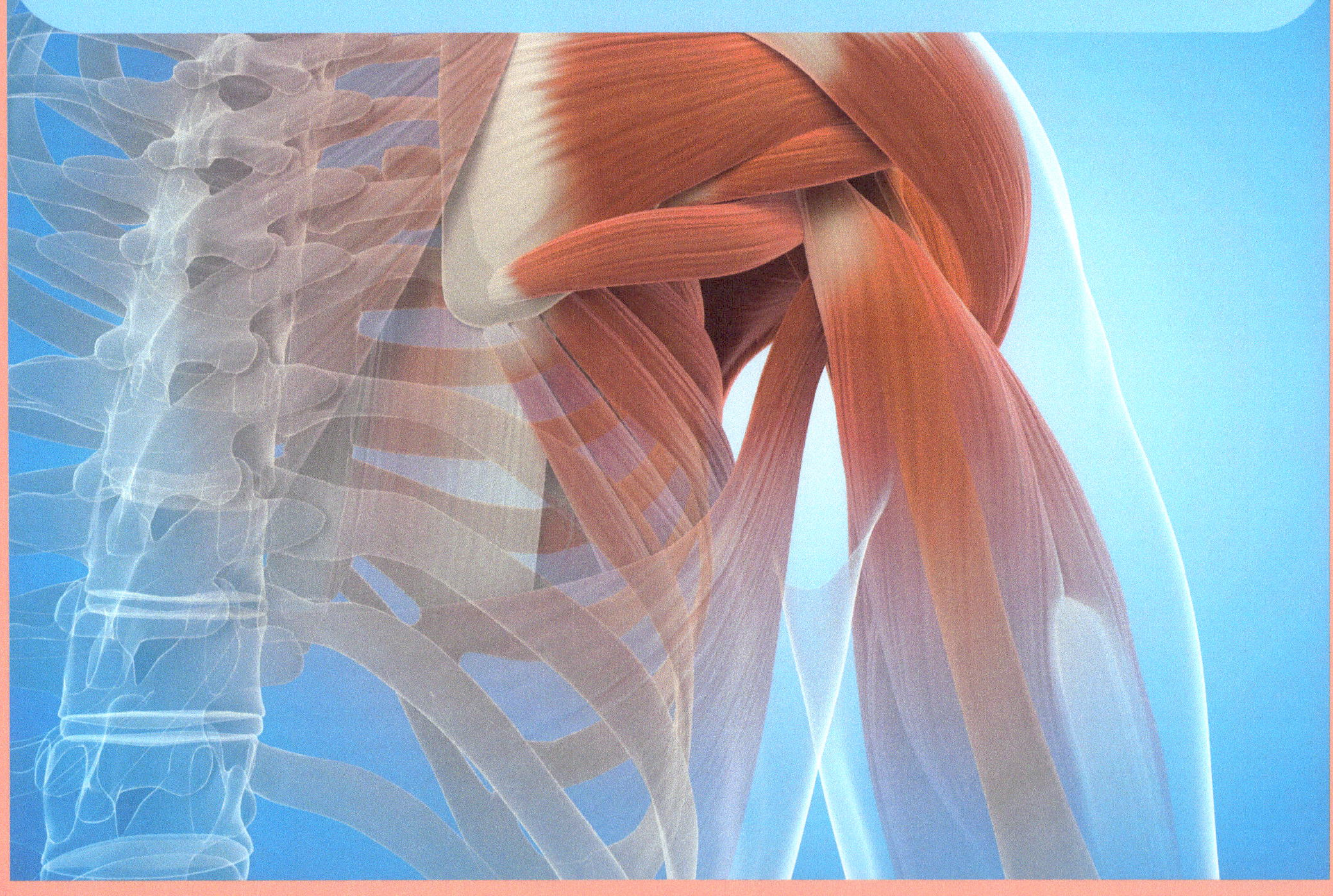

# N   Nausea

A feeling of sickness in the stomach which may cause you to vomit.

# O  Optometrist

A medical healthcare professional who cares for the eyes and eye health.

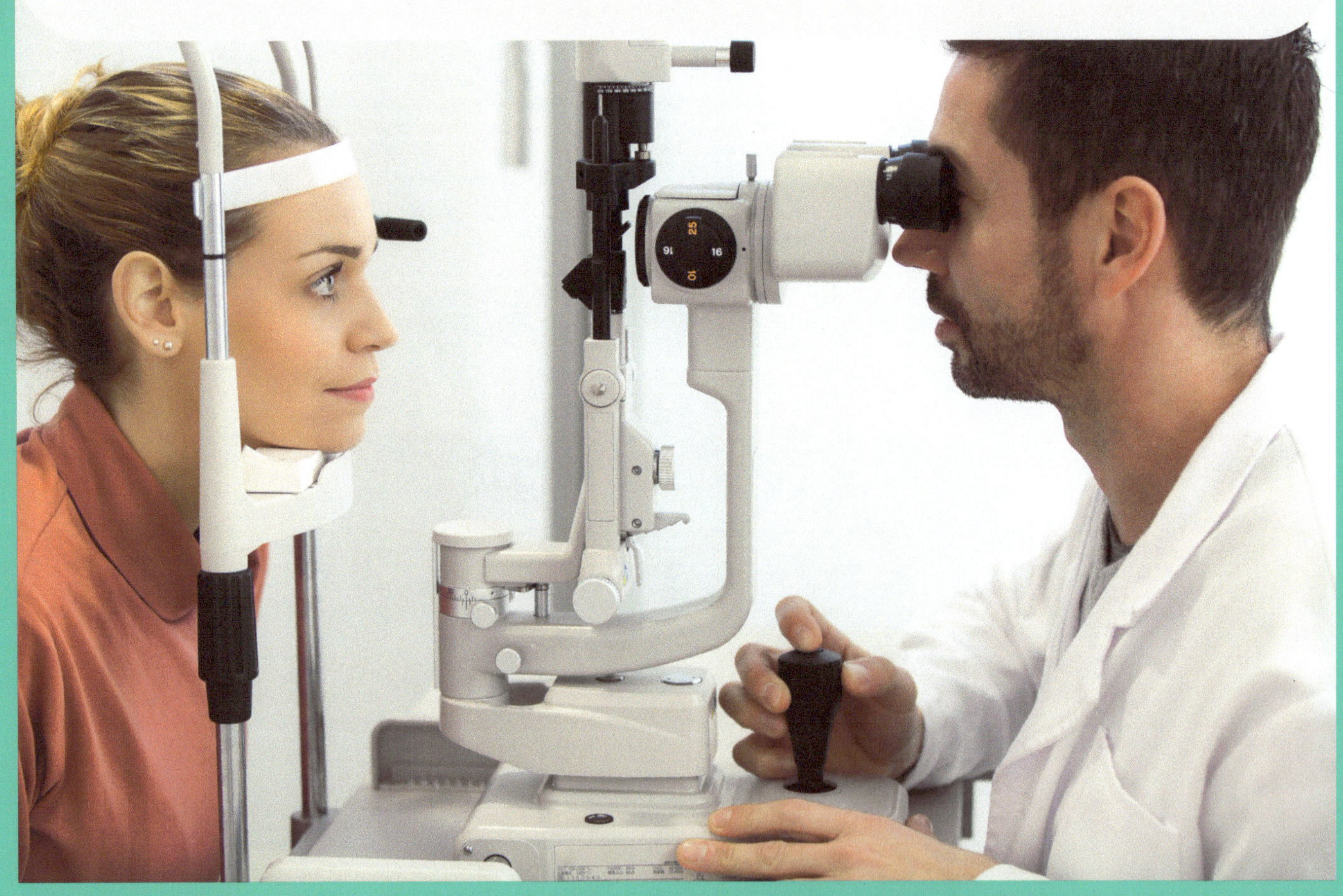

# P  Pulse

Rhythmic beating of the heart felt through the wrist or side of the neck.

# Q  Q Fever

Bacterial infection that can cause
flu-like symptons spread by animals.

# R Respiration

We breath in (inhale) oxygen and breath out (exhale) carbon dioxide.

# S  Stethoscope

A medical device used for listening to heartbeats and breathing.

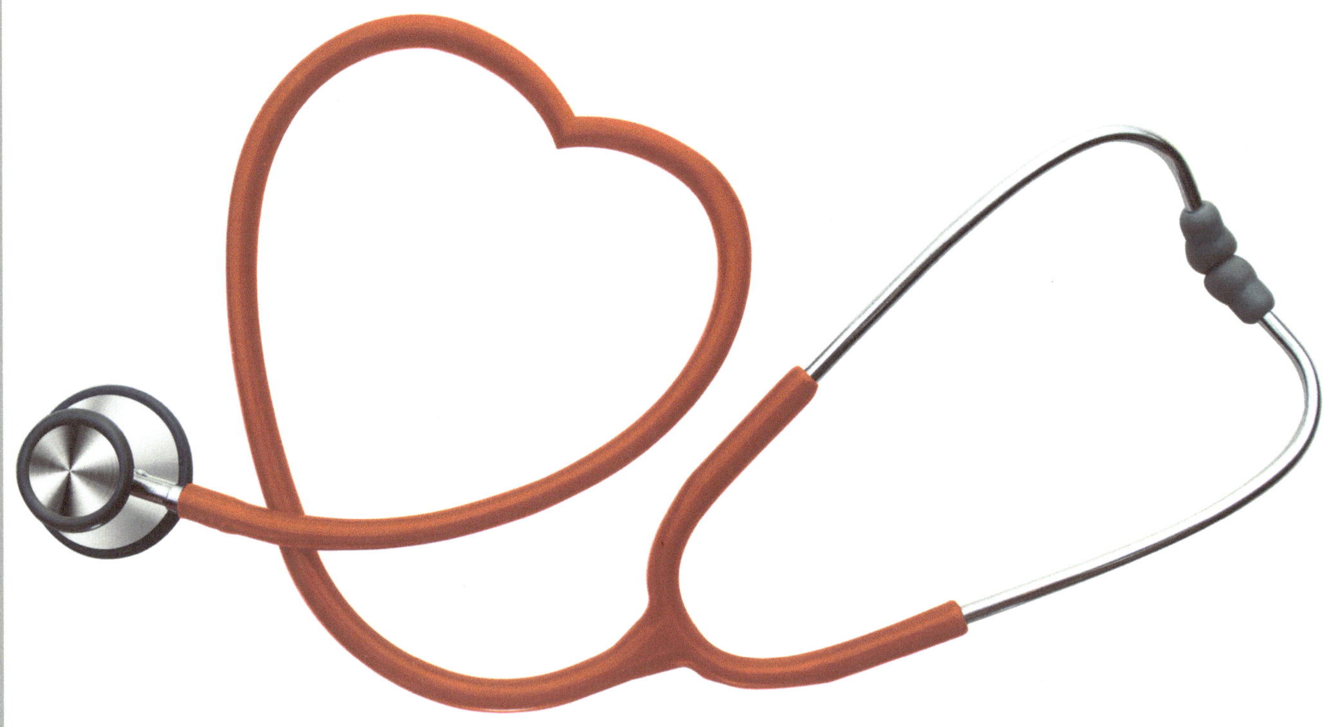

# T Tinnitus

A ringing or buzzing sound heard in the ear caused by various factors.

# U   Urine

The liquid waste product produced by the kidneys which is then excreted.

# V  Vital Signs

Taking blood pressure, temperature, weight; may indicate disease or illness.

# W  Water

Clear liquid you drink that makes up more than half of your body's weight.

# X  Xylitol

A natural sugar-free sweetener used in many products to replace sugar.

# Y  Yoga

Form of exercise involving stretching and breathing with health benefits.

# Z  Zika Virus

A viral infection spread by mosquitos marked by fever and rash.

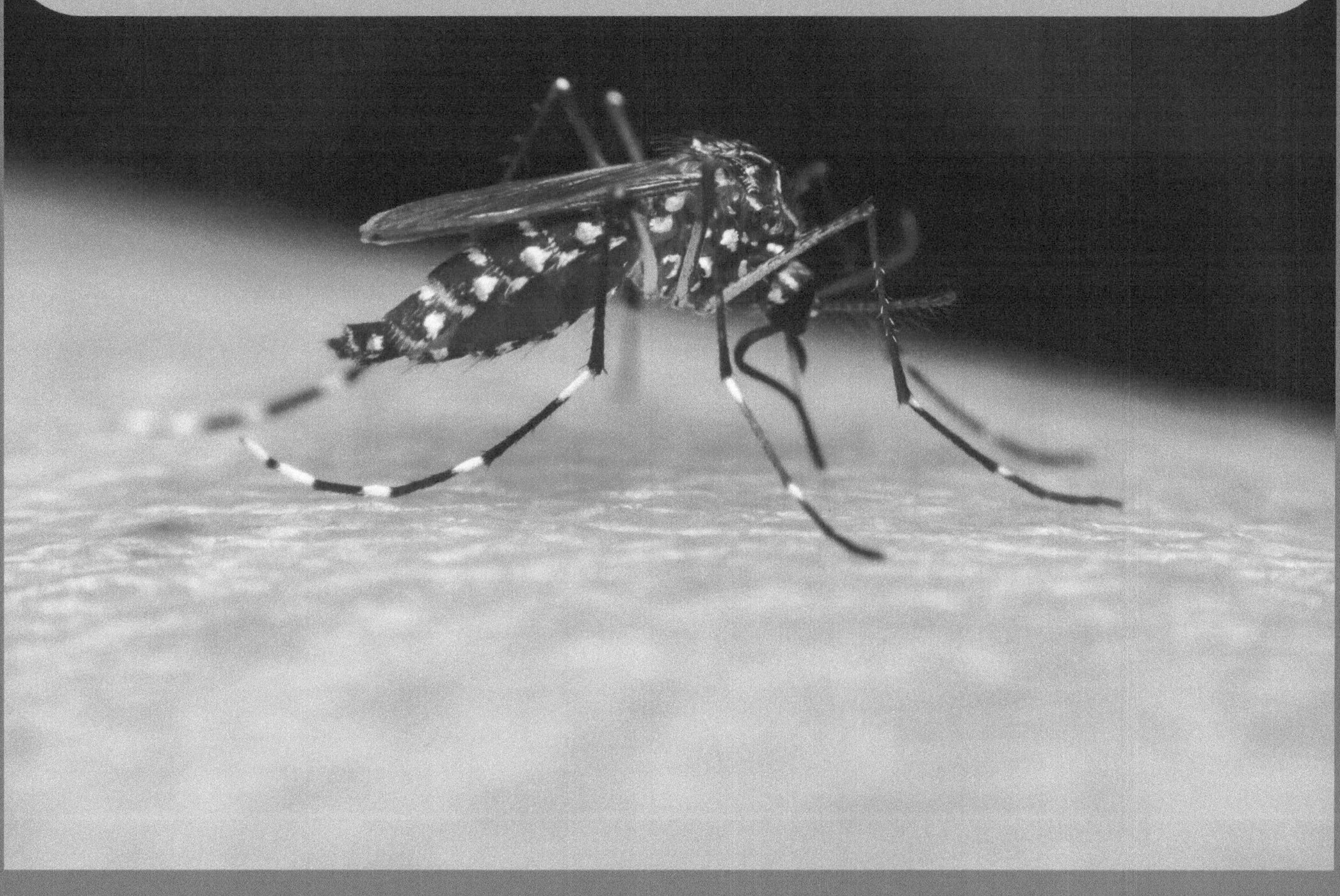

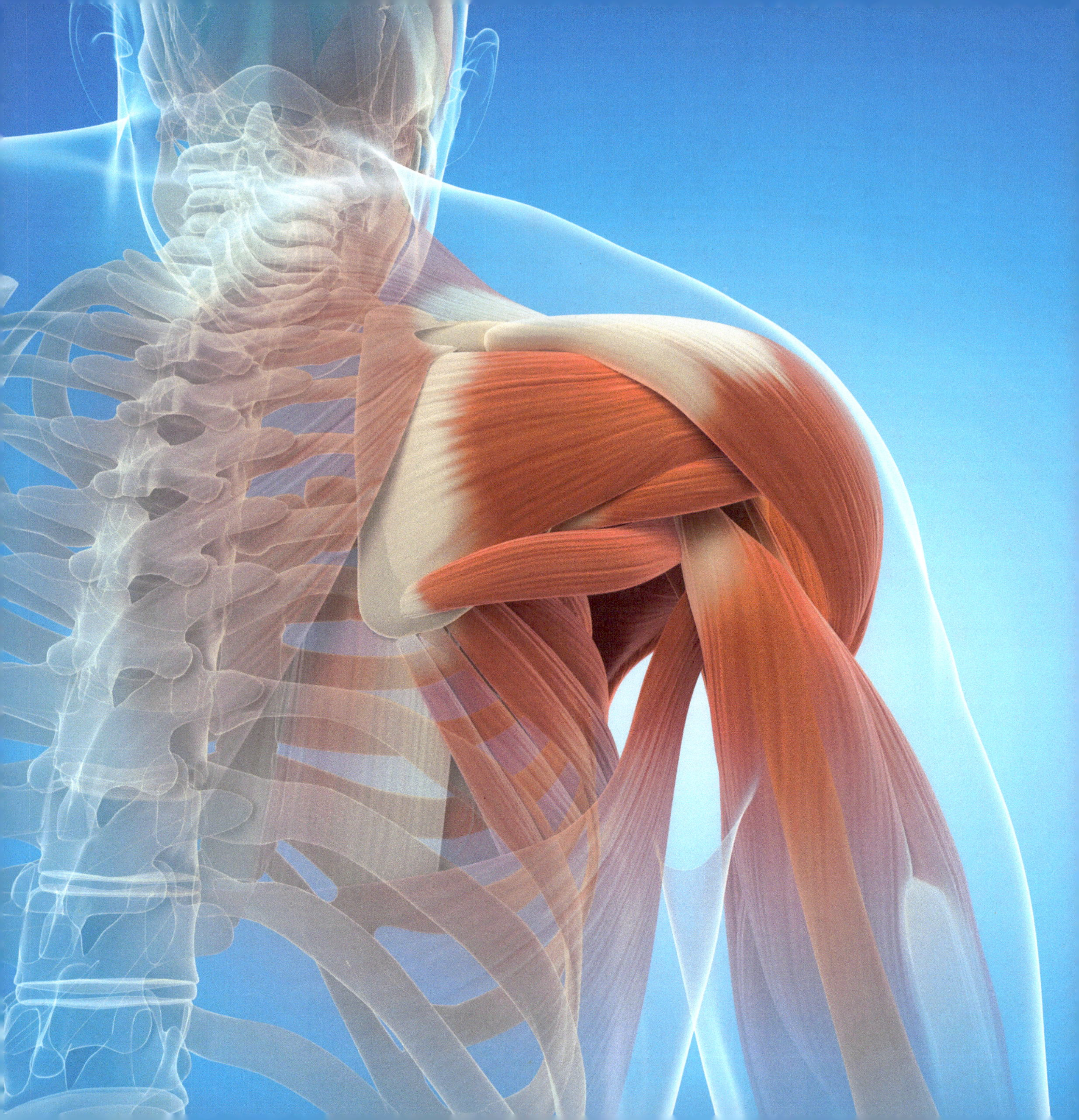

www.ingramcontent.com/pod-product-compliance
Lightning Source LLC
LaVergne TN
LVHW071659180726
843512LV00002B/489